Project Management
A Practical Handbook
English Edition

Written By
Raffaello Leti Messina

Credits

Cover by Alessandra Grossi

Copyright

Project Management – A Practical Handbook © 2013 by Raffaello Leti Messina all rights reserved under International and Pan-American Copyright Conventions.

Edition
1.5

First Edition

Digitally published on March 2013 on Amazon© Kindle© Store ASIN: B009WQ9JM8

Paperback Version published on February 2014 by Amazon©
ISBN-13: 978-1495976384
ISBN-10: 1495976386

Contents

- PREFACE 5
- INTRODUCTION 7
  - *Some Golden Rules* 10
- THE MANY ASPECTS OF THE PROJECT MANAGER 15
  - *The Internal Project Manager* 15
  - *The Initiating Project Manager* 16
  - *The Complete Project Manager* 17
- THE DOCUMENT MANAGEMENT LIFECYCLE 18
- BEFORE IMPLEMENTATION 21
  - *The Framework as a conceptual perspective* 21
- THE FRAMEWORK 24
  - *Context Description* 25
  - *Document Management* 25
  - *Communications Management* 25
- PROJECT SCOPE 26
  - *Assessment* 26
- PROBLEM DESCRIPTION (BUSINESS CASE) 28
  - *Defining the Objectives* 28
  - *Requirements/Requisites Definitions* 33
- SOLUTION DESCRIPTION 36
  - *Functional Description of Proposal* 36
  - *General Description of the Solution* 36
  - *Use Case Diagrams or Process Diagrams* 37
  - *Description of Functionalities or Features* 37
  - *Outline Representation of Solution* 39
  - *Defining Activities and Phases* 40
  - *Team Description* 45
  - *Cost Estimates/Financial Analysis* 45
  - *Constraints and Assumptions* 48
  - *Regulations and Standards Compliance* 48
  - *Criticalities and Attention Points* 50
  - *Risk Management* 51
- TECHNICAL DESCRIPTION OF THE SOLUTIONS 59
- EXECUTION PHASE 60
  - *Project Events* 60
  - *Meetings* 60
  - *Change Request e New Request* 65
  - *Tracking* 66
  - *Closing a Project* 69
- APPENDIX A: PSYCHOLOGY 70
- APPENDIX B: MANAGING TEAMS AND THE NEED TO EXPRESS ONE'S PERSONALITY 71

APPENDIX C – SUMMARY OF PROJECT DOCUMENTATION CONTENTS 74
APPENDIX D – CONNECTIONS BETWEEN BASIC ENTITIES AND PROJECT 75

BIBLIOGRAPHY 76

ABOUT THE AUTHOR 77

Preface

I agree! There is no need for a new usual book on Project Management!
There are already a myriad of publications that cover every aspect of each Project Management process, even the most unusual and debateable.

However, do you have a valid method for setting up your projects correctly?
Do you know how to create and share the documentation relating to each phase of the project in a rigorous, structured form?
Are you able to manage each fundamental step in a project lifecycle in a rigorous and structured way?
If you have answered *yes* to all three questions above, you don't need to read this book. If not...

This book is not intended to cover each aspect of the Project Management process in great depth and detail, but rather to provide a simple, clear guide to help the Project Manager set up the job effectively and consistently, with particular regard to the production and revision of the *Project Plan* and management of the project's documentation.

After some time leading projects of notable complexity during my professional career, I was faced with moving into a management and promotional role at the company and was faced with the problem of transferring my knowledge in the field of Project Management to those who would take over this work from me.
I had begun this process with a small number of colleagues and we decided to first formalize some useful rules for the Quality Control Manual for our business. We then realised that our focus on this formalization had overshadowed the content, and in the process of creating a broader vision of Project Management that also included the very earliest

phases of project conception, we decided to create this book, which also seemed worth publishing for a wider audience.

This is a book we would have liked to see in a bookshop when, over ten years earlier, we began to take our first steps in the field of project management and consultancy.

In fact, one of the primary goals of this text, is to move away from the widespread theoretical traditions of the existing texts in the field that also tend to abstraction, virtuosity and formalism, and provide a working method supported by a conceptual model, complete with analysis, examples, practical advices and template documents, relating to each of the key PM activities.

A book about what to do and how to do it, that is structured, rigorous, informed and transparent.

In order to increase the pragmatic value of the proposed method, this book provides examples on how to implement the approach to different kind of projects, from technological solutions to business processes design and optimization, and from constructions to *"Supply Chain"* initiatives.

Introduction

In the field of Project Management, the word Project refers to the product of a temporary organization of resources to be realized in a predefined time at a predefined cost.
The activities of overseeing, planning and coordinating project tasks, enabling their tracking as well as an effective communication among stakeholders are commonly referred to the Project Manager. Depending on his/her mandate/authority as well as on the organization and the very nature of the specific Project, PM's activities might include ensuring attainment of products to requirements, addressing issues and resolving conflicts that may arise among teams, influencing the budget management.

The title of Project Manager is too often bestowed, like an honorary title, attributed solely to the most important person in the company or institution hierarchy with an "unreasonably" broad interest in the project.
It also occurs, therefore, that the Project Managers are members of top management, burdened with the same title for an unfeasibly large number of projects, and who, in fact, simply do not have the possibility of following even one of them effectively.
This problem is not helped by the common practice of Team Leaders being at the same management level in the hierarchy and, therefore, prone to competing—even entering into outright conflict—with the Project Managers, in an attempt to emerge as the natural PM for the project, filling the void created by the absence of the Boss. The latter, inevitably quite early on in the project life cycle, ends up drowning in a myriad of distractions, having to intervene in conflicts, negotiate with his colleagues, separate the truth from conflicting reports on the above, or choose between antithetical visions of the same problem.

In reality, the bigger, more complicated and structured the project is, the closer the PM's job becomes a full time role, requiring a lot of work up-front and careful attention, impartiality, and experience, during the creation of the plan.

Furthermore, the diverse corporate or institutional organizations – be they horizontal or vertical – can have a major impact on the role of the PM and his prerogatives. These issues also affect the potential relationships between the PM and the organization's staff, resulting in very different levels of involvement and freedom.

In effect, one of the main difficulties for the Project Manager is the fact that it is not performed in the same way, nor does it always involve the same powers.

Rather than focusing on the person and prerogatives of the Project Manager, this text is a brief guide to the basic principles of Project Management, with the additional merit of providing a specific method.

This clarification also serves to puncture the myth of the Project Manager as a new professional in its own right, of the Guru, the 360º problem-solver, who fits into a specialist institute, but who does not fit into the reality of the complex and risky projects where a PM must learn to take advantage of valuable, effective sector collaborations.

Many aspects the Project Manager can assume at various points in the process are covered in more depth in the chapters covering Risk Management and Cost Management, areas in which, very often, the Project Manager must work in synergy with dedicated corporate structures.

The range of activities and topics that lead to good project management provides a framework that must have comprehensively benefit all the people with a legitimate involvement in the project – the *stakeholders*.

It matters little that these activities are the responsibility of a single individual – a rare situation in major projects – or, more frequently, handled by multiple persons. The important point is that the Project Manager knows how to present this framework clearly in a complete, holistic vision.

This framework is comprised of project documentation that must be clear, shared, with progressive technical detail, and fully consistent with the Objectives and Activities (Tasks).

The text illustrates:

- A framework for the creation of effective and thorough project documentation covering each phase of the same, from the declaration of needs, to the completion of the work, excluding none of the fundamental contents.

- A methodology for managing the key events that will inevitably occur during the project's lifecycle.

- A method for showing an evolutionary representation of the project's state and progression in a succinct, thorough and efficient form.

All of this has the goal of ensuring the Project Manager's activities remain exemplary even in the most difficult situations.

For the reasons detailed below, despite methodological support and experience, we do not believe in the convenience or expediency of retaining PMs who are incompetent in regard to project basics. Specifically, we do not believe the same person can effectively supervise the design and construction of, say, a dam, an innovative new vehicle, or a technical platform. However, we do believe in the applicability and value of our methods and principles.

Some Golden Rules

Transparency.
A matter of experience, but also an organizational challenge.

Projects often fail, either wholly, or in part, because the PM – or some Team Leader – has not acted transparently; perhaps by failing to make explain some of the project's limits, or analysis, or some error in the execution phase, in the hope that these problems will resolve themselves, or be solved by some divine intervention.
I like to say that this is an organizational problem.
The Project Manager is certainly one of the key people responsible for the success of the project, but he is not the only one. He cannot make incomplete specialised analyses magically become valid and exhaustive; he cannot verify every elaborate technical product for every part of the project.
The fact is that it is often the Project Manager who is the 'auteur' of the project, has an emotional connection with it – considers the project his 'baby'; but the Project Manager is nevertheless an employee of the company that is building the project, a factor that is inversely proportional to the cost of the project. Or he contends that, as a good Project Manager, he must make things work even when they cannot possibly work.
For some of these reasons, the Project Manager begins to acquire dangerous instinctive behaviours as early as the analysis phase, tending to minimize the cons and maximise the pros in each case.

The Project Manager must work in a transparent manner towards the organizations involved in the project and, in particular, towards the sponsors even, and especially, if this last is infamous for being a project killer. He must detect and signal every major problem, every deficiency, even those attributable to himself – obviously without

causing anxiety – sharing every relevant doubt and every unexpected piece of news with the stakeholders. Not doing so can lead to extremely grave, and maybe irreparable, consequences.
Therefore, the sponsor must choose a Project Manager who is not emotionally involved in the project.

A Project Manager who consistently acts with honesty and absolute transparency has a considerable likelihood of being appreciated even if the project should fail.

One relevant historical case study that taught me much, and which involved extraordinary numbers and high stakes, is that of Reginald H. Jones, who, once appointed of managing the computer division of General Electric, recommended to the board of this American colossus the sale of the division to Honeywell, to stop their losses that were, at the time, running to hundreds of millions of dollars. His position in regard to the project at G.E. to vie with IBM in the computer market did not allow Jones to remain director of the division, but led to his being given the position of CEO of what was then the biggest corporation in the world.

Scale, Complexity and Vagueness of the Objectives.
If a project has more than three or four objectives, it is usually possible, and desirable, to break it down into smaller projects.

If a project has objectives that are too vague, or too broad in scope – e.g. "provide housing sufficient for a population increase of several thousand", or "reduce production costs", it is already in trouble.
In such cases, it is better to talk of a program that will be practicable across multiple projects.
It is no coincidence that, in older disciplines, like construction, the concept of the project is generally clearer.
Too often, there is a tendency to identify a single project as the solution to a mix of problems or needs; this is a terrible way to begin!

The achievement of objectives must be measurable, and should be measured as soon as possible. It is best to provide precise methods for obtaining said metrics as soon as possible.

One easy option, where possible, is to create prototypes – *minimum viable product* – and verify their suitability in a structured way, that is: via the compilation of questionnaires by identified or potential users.

It is worth breaking the project down into logical phases. Each such phase requires suitable professionals. The following shows a sequence of such phases:

- **Analysis**
    - Description of Context
    - Description of Problem

- **Planning**
    - Outline Plan
        - Functional Definition of Solution

- o Working Plan
  - Technical Definition of Solution

- **Execution**

There being no single, unique, solution for each problem, the delicate and risky initial evaluation phase of the proposals merits.

In particular, there is no general solution for each problem, so the delicate and risky initial phase of evaluating the proposals requires skill and deep understanding, painstaking evaluations, and, usually, interdisciplinary approaches.

The outline and executive plans could be entrusted to different people, each of whom would bring different sensibilities to the process. This has produced notable successes in various fields, such as the manufacture of many automobiles of innovative design, where the designs were entrusted to specialists in each field. Or consider the construction of architectural masterpieces like the Sydney Opera House, the construction of which was a completely separate process from the competition in which its appearance was conceived.

Consider automobile manufacturing, where the designer is concerned with the attainment of one of the fundamental objectives to achieve the result, while also respecting the many design constraints. He initiates a process of refinement of both external and internal morphological characteristics, in accordance with the parameters of the components – chassis, motor, etc. – and thus with the other technicians and designers involved.
If a complex project is broken down into smaller components, each entrusted to highly specialised people,

the need for good management and project coordination is increased, but so is the probability of a good outcome.

Among the stakeholders, it is generally worth distinguishing, as clearly as possible, at least some entities – individuals or groups – according to the following list:

- The Sponsor or Financier
- The Project Manager – usually tasked with:
    - Coordinating stakeholders and conducting meetings
    - Managing project documentation and its maintenance
    - Risk Assessment
    - Research and promotion of alternative solutions
    - Control and documentation of project costs
- The Team Leaders – Those who are in charge of working groups charged with producing partial results
- The teams charged with the performance of activities or work packages

In a correctly defined project, these stakeholders must always remain distinct, with different influencing characteristics on the project's progress.
This does not always happen.

The Many Aspects of the Project Manager

As already discussed, the role of the Project Manager does not always imply the same prerogatives.
In a well-defined project, the Project Manager's mandate has clearly defined duties and limits. This mandate can have very different limits, ranging from roles closer to that of an *advisor*, or a coordinator, to that of a manager responsible for the correct flow of the process in order to produce the desired results – from conception to conclusion of the project.
It is generally possible to identify the following types of Project Manager, each with its pros and cons...

The Internal Project Manager
It is common for businesses and institutions to choose a Project Manager from within their own organisation. This may seem the best solution.

Strengths	Weaknesses
Highest sensitivity to the problem.	Complex management of links with colleagues and possible impact from old grudges
Easier links with sponsors and stakeholders	There is a risk of narrower vision and avoidance of disruptive innovation due to an inherent conditioning in favour of retaining the "*status quo*"

The Initiating Project Manager

This type of Project Manager is usually from one of the suppliers – often the main, or only one. The Project Manager will be the one who came up with the initial project proposal and will therefore have a strong emotional investment in the project, often to the point of being unable to admit the possibility of flaws in the initial plan requiring correction or outright elimination.

Strengths	Weaknesses
Extremely invested in the success of the project	Complexities in the management of relationships with the client's operations, and difficulties in having the legitimacy of his role accepted
	Requires notable skills in negotiation and communication
	Likely to be interested in the solution's economic worth, while tending not to reveal *hidden costs*

The Complete Project Manager

External to the organisation, this Project Manager is not merely an expression of one or more suppliers, and has experience in the management of similar projects. This is similar to the Works Manager position in the construction industry, representing the interests of the sponsors, with the difference that he can be hired to manage either or both the design and construction phases.

Strengths	Weaknesses
Emotionally detached, giving greater likelihood of supervisory transparency and efficiency	Complexity in managing ties with the client's operations, and difficulties in ensuring their role's authority if the appointment is weak
Objectivity in resolving disputes and evaluating proposals	Needs to be highly skilled in negotiation and communication
Impartiality when reporting to the Sponsor	

The Document Management Lifecycle

The project documentation is designed to be shared, to ensure timely contributions and continuous checks.
This represents an opportunity for summarizing, and for controlling the choices and "pacing" of the project.
Often, a project is subject to many modifications; its content expands, with new objectives and / or requirements added through various vicissitudes; and strategic directions may change.
As a project cannot be considered the property of those who initiate it, or who participate in it, but is more typically under the aegis of an organisation – be it large or small – interested in its outcome, it is therefore fundamental, even for the protection of those who work on it, that it is possible to revise the project.
For this to be possible, it is necessary for the project documentation to be well organised and that each document provides for the option to identify when substantial modifications to the same were made.

The project documentation is often comprised of a multitude of individual documents: reports, interviews, presentations, detailed analyses, etc.
During the lifecycle of a project there are at least three potentially critical turning points relating to the three primary figures: the Sponsor, the Project Manager, and the Team Leader.
One of the conditions for preventing such turning points causing severe trauma to the project – and to ensure the management is appreciated – is to ensure it is provided with complete, effective documentation.

For project documentation to be effective, it must meet the following three characteristics:

1. It must comprise a "limited" number of documents – in particular, it must include the *master plan*, the

structure of which is described in more detail below. This document must always be kept up-to-date, and be written so as to be comprehensible to the project's top management and acting as a form of summary.

2. Each of the few documents describing the entire project must evolve with the project itself, documenting – as part of the document's name itself – the *release* (or version) number, as well as the date of addition / modification of every Objective, Requirement, Function or Risk.

3. The documentation must provide a detailed list of all significant appendices, each with its issuing date, and with particular attention given to documents that have led to the introduction or modification of any Objectives, Requirements, Functions, or Risks

The management will greatly appreciate the time saved in being able to read such a condensed set of documents in order to understand the state of the works and the reasons for any changes.

The most common practice for project documentation management is a stile we can define as "Italian legislation", in which a legal measure modifies a large number of articles in earlier measures, producing inefficient and annoyingly labyrinthine results.

Furthermore, any documentation that adheres to the characteristics described is of great value in justifying circumstances without having to produce laborious reconstructions. The result is an efficient division of labour and appropriate assumptions of responsibilities.

It goes without saying that, for the purpose of providing the depth necessary, the documentation should have a hypertext structure and made available either on an intranet or the Internet.

Warning: a project document must have a reasonable overall development, in proportion with the complexity and scale of the operations; management should reward the ability to express oneself concisely and effectively.

Before Implementation

The Framework as a conceptual perspective

A good project begins by identifying clear and simple objectives.
This is easier said than done.
Each objective will have a variable number of requirements and restrictions, compliance with which means the objective has been met.
The tricky phase of determining the Objectives and Requirements, is the definition of the terms of the project's problem and, as such, should not include aspects that provide a specific solution. The latter is crucial: it means we can focus on the problems without prematurely limiting or restricting the project planning and design options.

Once the problem has been defined in terms of Objectives and Requirements, we can then move onto the definition and selection of a solution.
The solution will often comprise multiple elements. These will include functions that are key to solving the problem. Henceforward, it will be more appropriate to talk in terms of functions while the term 'operation' will be reserved primarily for elements of the general operational framework of a business or organisation.

The functions are performed via a series of Activities or Tasks that form the Work Breakdown Structure – WBS – representing the decomposition of the work into individual activities.
Figure 1 shows a diagram of this important classification of the fundamental components of the project, highlighting their role in describing the problem, or the solution.
The hardest task the Project Manager is likely to face is in the deconstruction of the work and quantification necessary for carrying out basic individual tasks.

The following paragraphs are structured like a project document. Each one describes considerations, advice and, above all, the description of the contents that said paragraph should include in your project.

The diagram proposed for the project documentation's structure also documents the key phases of the Project Management process and hints at the compilation and updating of a project document that could be defined as the *Master Plan*. It is more than a charter, but less than the whole of the documentation, that represents a summary of the story and state of the project, providing a complete, continuous, overview of the same for management.

Therefore, the extent of this document must be limited as far as possible, yet capable of providing the big picture.

From this, it is strongly recommended to write and release the documentation with hypertext links to more general documentation as well as those providing specific in-depth analysis.

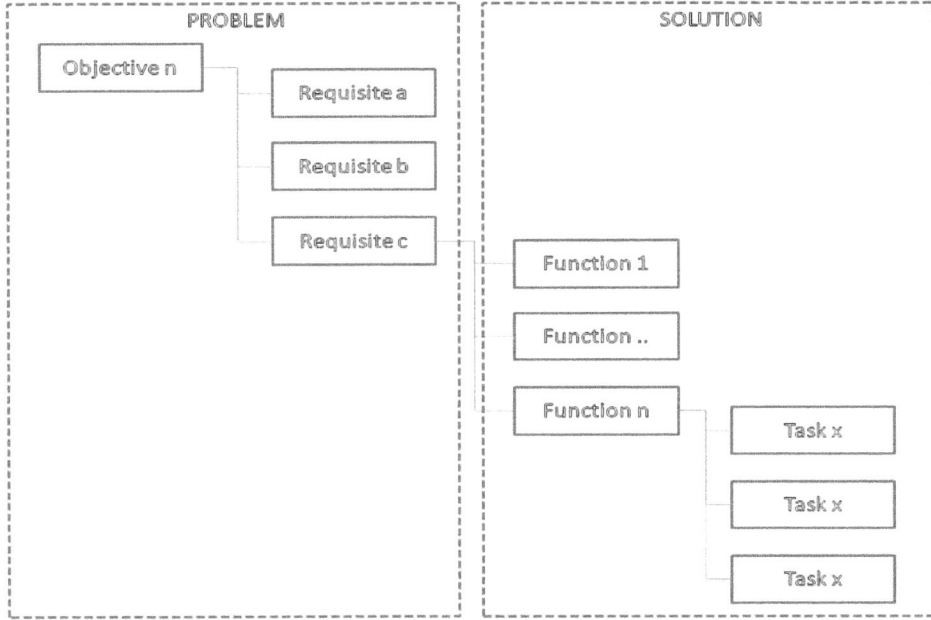

Picture 1

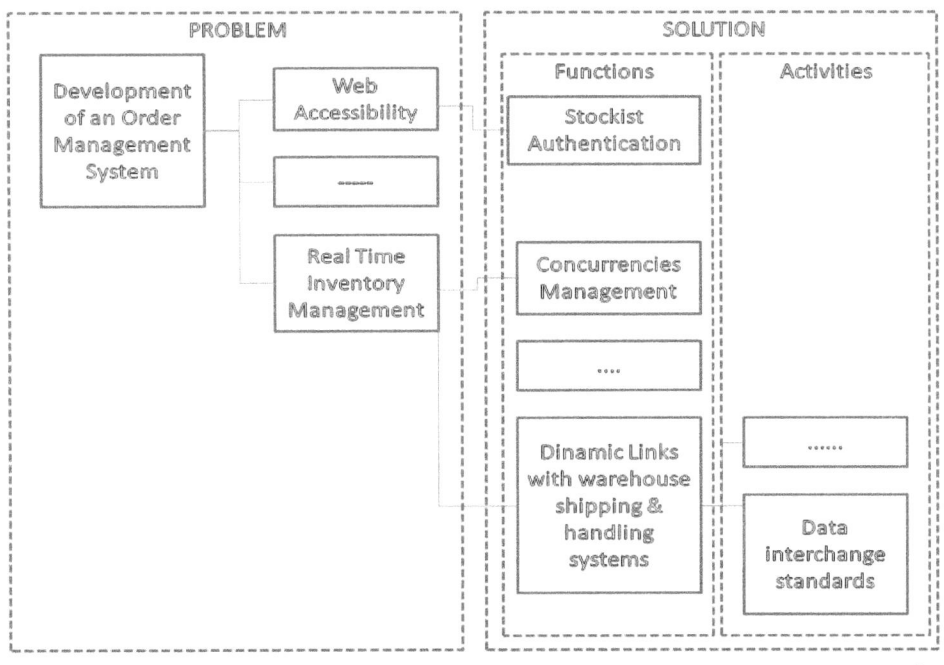

Picture 2

THE FRAMEWORK

The following paragraphs are already a breakdown of the project documentation, with a particular emphasis on hierarchically linking together conceptual pieces of the project description or design.

Context Description

In this section we include every relevant observation regarding the operational context, any external restrictions affecting the project, etc.

It is also worth explaining the genesis of the project, the promoters, and the relationships between business operations at the time when the initiative was launched.

Document Management

This includes a section describing the project documentation management process.

Existing technologies provide extraordinarily efficient tools for managing and, above all, sharing the documentation, and for project communication.

It is good practice in this section for the Project Manager to explain, to all the professionals involved, the guidelines for the storage, sharing, approval, and organisation of the project documentation.

Communications Management

A project in progress can involve a sizeable amount of communication that will become an integral part of the project's documentation.

In many cases, distribution of information can be disorganised or indiscriminate, usually producing negative effects.

All communications, throughout the lifetime of the project, must flow, and be managed, according to a plan. This plan must be defined in this section of the Project Plan, on which great emphasis must be placed. Specifically, the section relating to Communications Management will include:

- Communications classification – calling of meetings, presentations, issues, minutes.

- Each type of communication has an associated distribution list; that is, the recipients to which that type of communication will be sent.

Generally, the Project Manager must be the nexus of these communications, as well managing them using an appropriate, well organised, *repository*.

Communications that are internal to individual work teams can follow their own flows, which may be spontaneous, or defined by the team leaders.

Project Scope

Assessment

The *assessment* refers to the description of each element explaining the current situation in relation to the problems that are intended to be resolved through implementation of the project, as well as each important element that could influence the outcome.

For projects aimed at improving some organisational practices within an organisation, for example, it is necessary to describe the current practices, taking care to detail only the areas that are strictly relevant to the objectives.

For construction projects, it may be worthwhile – for example, to describe the state of the authoritative processes – the elements regarding the financing options available, etc.

In short, the assessment section should provide a photograph of the current position, highlighting all the elements that have led to the decision that the project is needed.

Problem Description (Business Case)

A brief definition of the problems or the core achievements of the initiative will precede the following paragraphs.

In case of a product or a technology solution you'd better introduce in a very short way which problems the project development is expected to mitigate or which relevant advantages it will bring.

Paraphrasing Mies Van der Rohe in this case "less will be more", the more concise way to describe the benefits of the initiative will surely be the most effective.

Although the definition is usually not welcome by NGOs or no-profit organizations, this section is also often referred to as "Business Case".

Defining the Objectives

The Objectives of a project comprise the mandate for action and must therefore have the following characteristics:

- They must be defined clearly, precisely, and concisely

- No objective can repeat, either in whole or in part, any other objective

- Objectives must be measurable

- Objectives must be attainable in a specific timeframe and within budget

"Creating an efficient telecommunications network", "Building a beautiful theatre", or "Improving citizens' quality of life" are not valid objectives: they are two general as to the underscored terms do not correspond a defined measure or criteria.

To represent the Objectives, we propose using the tabular format shown below.

Objective #n Description	
Aspects to be included in the scope of the Project:	
Out-of-scope aspects:	
Comments:	
Date:	
Docs:	

Where:

Description is a brief description of the objective.

Aspects to be included in the scope of the Project: lists all the elements that will help reach the objective's goal and will be influenced by the project activities. These aspects are those that, according to the objective's description, must all be resolved before said objective can be met.

Aspects to be excluded from the Project's scope: Out-of-scope elements are those that will not be considered as part of the initiative. In some cases, this exclusion is not due to the irrelevance of such aspects, but to the necessity of limiting Project complexity by acting on priorities and therefore they might be included within the scope of a subsequent initiative. By way of explanation, consider this example: A wholesale retail business decides to build a new web-based system for booking deliveries, to improve efficiency for their clients, without changing the charging, rates or billing management processes. For this example, the entry for this field could be: "Every aspect relating to accounting and administration".

Comments – every note related to the aspects to be analysed in greater depth, or inspection / checks to be performed.

Date – is the date when the Objective was introduced or modified

The following line, **Docs** field, is reserved, where necessary, for a list of project documents – usually meeting minutes, management / sponsor interviews – that prove the necessity or need of the Objective. The entries on said list should be links to documents available on the network.

Problem Description and Objectives, together with key roles and primary measures, or (better) in some cases the expected trend of Project's primary measures, should better be synthesized within one or maximum two pages in the so called "Project Charter". Such synthesis provides a solid, clear-enough snapshot of the project that is generally highly appreciated by top-management as it also provides the foundation for Project's Performance Management.

Here is a sample Project Charter.

Picture 3

Valid examples of primary measures are:
- A process lead-time, such as the time needed to process a document.
- The unit cost of a product or a part.
- The overall cost of a service.
- The available working floor.
- The number of items delivered per hour.
- The gallons of water provided.
- The customer satisfaction.
- Total sales.

In any case, bear in mind that the more Objectives and their degree of achievement are measurable, the more a Project is traceable and likely to succeed.
Therefore, the prior definition of unequivocal performance metrics is crucial to Project success.

The Project Charter might include the definition of key secondary measures (and their range or trend) that should ensure the respect of primary measures trends.

Secondary measures are those from which primary measures depend.

In example, if the one of the Project Objectives is "To increase Customer Satisfaction..." concerning a customer support service, then the primary measure is a somehow gauged Customers' Satisfaction, and one out of other valid secondary measure might be the expected trend of the standard deviation of trouble-ticket resolution times.

Requirements/Requisites Definitions

There are two fundamental goals for this section:

- Identify, clearly and succinctly, the requirements of the work.

- Highlight, clearly and directly, the functions needed to attain one (or more) objectives

The requirements define the properties or characteristics that the work, resulting from the project, should provide.
Example 1: A software development project.
The requirements might be:

- Content and operating constraints of each graphical user interface.

- Needs, compatibilities and restrictions regarding the connection or exchange of data with other systems involved.

- Specifications for security and user access profiles for the system.

Example 2: An architectural project for a new theatre.
The requirements might include:

- Total budget available or total cost of the work.

- Seating capacity.

- Provisional number and location of main entrances and exits.

- Number and specifications of parking areas.

- Refreshment areas (if any) and their dimensions.

Note that requisites are rarely defined solely by the client. For example, constraints due to local regulations, as well as technical requirements, form implicit requirements in their own right.
These are non-explicit requirements, which are fundamental, but not always obvious.
This means the Project Manager must know how to assess the completeness of these outline requirements.
This is one of the reasons why we believe a Project Manager is not interchangeable across projects in completely different disciplines where he lacks a relevant experience.

The definition of requirements is probably the trickiest part of the entire project. It must be derived either directly, or indirectly, from statements made by the client – sponsor – or persons qualified to articulate said requirements.
For project proposals, and in emphasising their value, it will be well worth differentiating between the proposed requirements, those arising from autonomous analysis of the problems, and those directly inferable from the requirements given by the client.
In each case, the link between requirements and objectives must be made clear. This tends to avoid the proliferation of requirements, however tempting, that are not connected to the project's objectives and thus worthless, misleading, and often inappropriate with regard to the project's goals.

To represent the requirements, we propose the following tabular format:

ID	Description	OU	Referenced Documents	Obj.	Date

Where:

ID is the identifier code for the requirement. It is advisable to assign this using a format that relates to the Function (described shortly). For example, a requirement expressed by the client could have an ID of RQ_CL01.

The **Description** field contains a brief description of the requirement – need, or operating constraint.

The **OU** field is intended to indicate the client's internal organisational unit that proposed the need or requirement – e.g. 'Administration & Finance' or 'Operations & Logistics', or 'Information Systems'.

The **Referenced Documents** field lists the documents that formed the basis for the requirement – meeting minutes, interview reports, etc.

The **Obj.** field shows the objective to which the requirement is related.

The **Date** field reports the date when the requirement was added or modified.

The requirements are therefore the true parameters for the solution.

Solution Description

Functional Description of Proposal

This section is potentially dedicated to everyone. It is primarily aimed at presenting a project to *top management*.
The functional description of a project proposal must be:

- Succinct
- Clear and comprehensive to a lay reader
- Provided with meaningful graphical illustrations

A good Project Manager must ensure this part of the document is comprehensible by all, while also being as concise as possible.

General Description of the Solution

The outline description of the proposal must be relatively short and not include any opinions about said proposal.

In situations where there are multiple proposals, the description should provide the salient elements that have led to the proposal described becoming the preferred option.
This section must highlight how the proposal will meet all the project objectives, with explicit reference to the descriptions of same, compliance with specified requirements, and with explicit references also to the latter.

The dates of the presentation and approval of the proposal must also be reported, as well as the dates of any substantial variations or changes to the same.

Use Case Diagrams or Process Diagrams

In most cases, a project results in usable products, albeit usable in different ways by different categories of clients.
The IT examples in the use case chart offer an immediate check of requested functionality. The plans for a project for a new hospital allows for documenting accessibility and logical separation of various flows.
It is absolutely crucial to include a section dedicated to documentation regarding the use of the product.
If the project concerns production processes, or more generally, business processes, there are several ways of decomposing and charting them in order to represent different qualitative and quantitative characteristics and their interaction with external elements.
Some examples are Process Maps or Cross-Functional Process Maps, where the so-called swim lanes provide evidence of the interactions among different actors or business functions, or even SIPOC Diagrams (Supplier, Input, Process, Output, [Requirements]). These are also design tools that provide a useful snapshot of what the result of the Project will be and should be included in an executive summary.

Description of Functionalities or Features

The definition of functions provides an overview of the fulfilment of the needs expressed by Objectives and Requirements.
The functions are connected to Requirements and Objectives, as shown in Fig. 1.
Obviously, a function may meet more than one requirement and, occasionally, more than objective. Their representation of can use a tabular format with the following data:

ID	Description	Reference Documents	Obj.	Requirements	Date

If a function cannot be linked to one or more objectives and requirements, it is to be considered either unnecessary, or the lists of objectives and requirements are incomplete.

Outline Representation of Solution

A general representation of the solution – a simulation or a model in the case of a construction project, or car; an intuitive and graphically enjoyable diagram for a technical project, or a high level process map – is a fundamental tool for communicating the idea to a non-technical audience, such as top management, who often represent the Sponsor.
Force yourself to present the solution in a single "design" and exercise your critical faculties when checking it for clarity and simplicity.

If there are formal techniques in the design process applicable to either all or part of the solution, this is not the time to use them.

The content of this section is not a presentation for technicians, so any semantic virtuosity will not be appreciated. In fact, any attempt to add technical content to the presentation will be considered a fussy, malicious attempt to show off your skills.

Defining Activities and Phases

Here, we describe the path towards the final result, through a breakdown of the work into macro activities – *work packages* – and then, into atomic activities, called *tasks*, using a progressively deeper analysis of the details.
The output of this definition phase of the activities is a hierarchical list in tabular format, known as WBS ("Work Breakdown Structure") similar to that shown below:

ID	Activity	Team	ID of Preliminary Activities	Estimated Duration

One of the principal qualities of the Project Manager is his capacity to check every individual activity is effectively atomic – that is, tasks with a minimum duration and, for the most part, relating to a single resource.
This is why the estimate, in terms of duration and work needed to complete the task, is more credible the more it has been broken down and decomposed. Thus the following examples...

- Redesign of all user interfaces
- Excavations of construction lots

... do not represent elementary activities for a correct WBS and therefore the work and resources needed for their completion and determining their duration would not be credible. Such activities are insufficiently detailed.

Do not use a paragraph to present a single WBS.
The breakdown of the work should be documented, justified and subdivided by area, or at least into functional modules and *work packages*.

One of the most common and effective methods for presenting the chronology of activities and, therefore, the work phases, is to use a Gantt chart.

As said, elementary elements contained in a WBS are commonly referred to as Tasks. In order each Task to be completed it will require a specific amount of resources. Although, in order to ensure Task atomicity, its belonging to only one human resource is recommended, a variable amount of other type of resources would be necessary, such as equipment, software or spaces, each of which may have a fixed or variable cost.

The sum of Tasks individual cost, stemming from applied resources unitary cost, extended to the duration of Task, will correspond to Project overall cost, which could be confronted to cost trends while tracking activities along their development.

The following exhibit shows a simple GANNT chart with tasks, predecessor constraints, baseline traces, and current task timing.

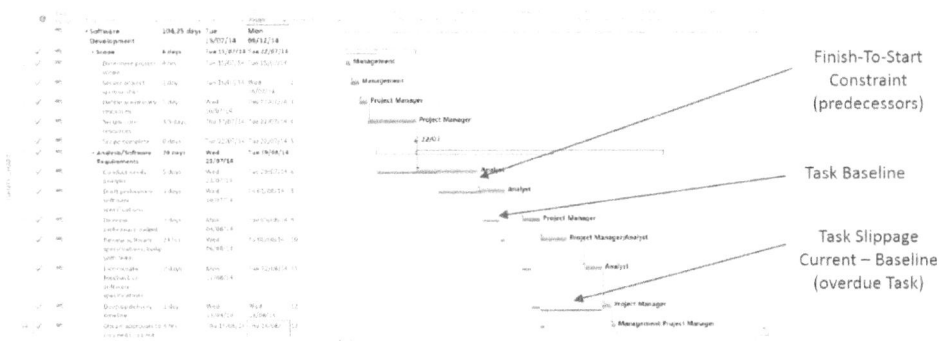

Picture 4

In each case, especially where there are uncertainties regarding the exact completion times for individual activities, it is advisable to create a PERT ("Program Evaluation and Review Technique") diagram.

Invented at the end of the 1950s within the Polaris Project of the US Navy, the PERT is a "network diagram" or directed graph in which the connections or arcs represent the prerequisite nature of the activities, and the nodes represent the individual activities themselves. Originally, this was reversed, with the nodes representing milestones and the lines the activities, but the effect is the same. The nodes are associated with a minimum time (Optimistic Time), a maximum duration (Pessimistic Time) and the expected duration for the completion of the task (Most Likely Time).

For each activity, the time taken to complete it is estimate as follows:

Expected Time = (Optimistic Time + 4 x Most Likely Time + Pessimistic Time) / 6

It is then possible to produce a graph as shown below, the tracing of which, starting from one of the initial activities and ending at the node representing the end of the project, provides an estimate of the probable duration of the whole sequence.

It is also possible to show graphically the *Critical Path*, which is the longest path to reach the end of the project, starting from a particular initial activity. This is extremely useful for identifying individual activities that directly affect the maximum duration of the project, and those that can be delayed without influencing the project's overall duration.

Sample PERT Chart. Nodes represent Tasks and their expected duration in days. Arrows indicate precedence between tasks.

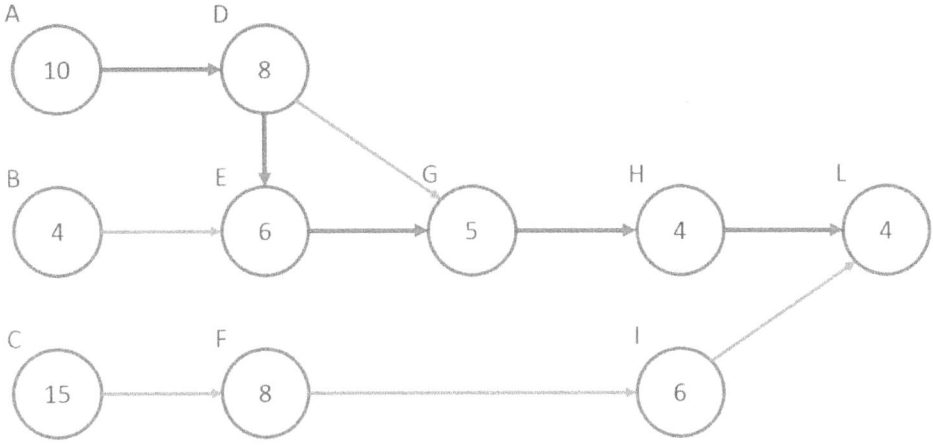

Tasks on Critical Path: A-D-E-G-H-L
Project expected duration: 37 days

Picture 5

The widest red arrows indicate the *Critical Path*, passing through the five tasks labelled, respectively, A, D, G, H and L, and representing a total duration of 28 days for completion of all the activities.
It is important to note that, if possible, adding more resources to tasks on the critical path is the only way to shorten the overall duration of the project.
In fact, by definition, adding more resources to activities other than those located on the critical path will not result in a shorter project or reduced slippage risk.
Therefore, tasks on the critical path are also viewed as project constraints.
According to Goldratt's Theory of Constraints, adding more resources to critical tasks may result in changes in the critical path as new constraints may arise. The iterative process of configuring different additive resource allocations, which in turn result in different critical paths, is

obviously constrained by project budget as well as by the very nature of individual tasks and resources.

It is also important to keeping the PERT graph up-to-date during the project in order to review the program and set any necessary corrective actions in motion.

Today, there are various computer-based tools for automating the production of PERT diagrams and identifying the Critical Path.

Team Description

This section should consist only of a list of names and surname.
Its purpose is to document and verify, even if only at a sectorial level, the adequacy and completeness of competencies involved.
For this purpose, and as a function of each group of activities, the description must justify the size and composition of the teams, with particular regard to leadership figures.
To this end, it is necessary to show: the name of the team, its area of competence and intervention, the names and qualifications of team leaders, and names and qualifications of team members.

Cost Estimates/Financial Analysis

The cost of a project is clearly a property of the chosen design solution.
This solution, when being written up in a suitably detailed Project Plan is, therefore, already chosen.
However, the total cost depends on the costs of human resources, the costs of tools, facilities and infrastructure, the time required to implement the solution, local taxation, and on its inherent risks. A proper cost analysis must also cover not only certain costs, but potential costs that may arise as well.
In light of this, the Sponsor of relatively expensive projects may commission multiple *Project Plans*, in order to obtain a more reliable and comprehensive comparative analysis of the costs and benefits of different solutions.
It is worth remembering that the decision-making process that results in the selection of a particular solution involves assessments of business strategy deployment that are outside the scope of Project Management.

Although the cost is likely to be of much interest to the reader of a project proposal, it is frequently placed at the end of the *Project Plan*, given its necessary and suitable references to the components of the project solution chosen for implementation.

Frequently, this section is not even part of the *Project Plan* released to most of the stakeholders, being irrelevant to the goal of understanding the project and likely to start debates and assessments that the Sponsor does not wish to share.

Its location at the end of the *Project Plan* is thus motivated by the need to justify and support said costs, making explicit reference to available equipment and human resources defined as necessary in the definition of the proposal.

Cost estimates must therefore be modular, documenting the possibility of progressive investments, each of which must be supported by explicit references upon achievement of partial results.

Obviously, the cost estimates may be subject to changes. The Project Manager has the duty to report these in this section, taking care to highlight the date and reason for the change for each component of the cost.

The process of authorizing budget variations in face of change/new requests or changing environmental conditions may vary depending on organization and/or project type. According to the PRINCE2 framework, cost tolerances should be defined prior the project start and obviously linked to the expected benefits described within the Business Case. Within such tolerances the Project Manager may act autonomously authorizing budget variations, while in case the variation exceed the allowed limit, she/he must refer to the Project-Board for authorization.

Such practice is common to many organizations except for that any project's budget variation, especially relevant ones are discussed and analyzed collegially with the contribute of various stakeholders. Relevant budget variations, often due to changed environmental conditions, may require global revision of the Project Plan and/or validation from accountant or financial experts; and these experts may ask the project teams in order to evaluate different alternatives and hypotheses.

Cost estimate should be broken down into phases and, for each phase, into resources – human resources, infrastructures, plants, licenses, tools, taxes, etc.

For almost every project, this section should include a Breakeven Analysis. The Break Even Analysis is a very important verification tool.

Such formalized analysis checks the conditions and the time needed in order to obtain the return of investment. The point in time when the overall initiative cost will equal the related benefits is called breakeven point. Like every forecast whose formulation is based on cost and potential returns or earnings decomposition it requires great experience and vertical skills. Therefore, it is normally performed by experts, and those who are not familiar with it are strongly encouraged to recur to experts advice and validation at least. In case the subject of the Project is the launch of a new product or service, delegating the Breakeven Analysis to an expert marketer is probably the best choice to spare yourself a poor figure.
To gain familiarity with Breakeven Analysis, carefully pick sources and refer to previous established works related to similar projects.

In the public and no-profit sectors however, due to the complexity of implications and interdependencies, estimating project's prospective benefits may be so difficult that virtually no PM alone is able to perform a sound Breakeven Analysis. In such cases, multidisciplinary teams are engaged in a complex somehow iterative process that frequently results in the depiction of different scenarios that will imply a careful monitoring of some key environmental variables as well as the attentive tracking of the impacted key performance indicators as the project progresses.

Constraints and Assumptions

Every project has fixed points – elements that are non-negotiable – and which must therefore be presented as such.
Also shown should be any processes and assumptions that affect the dynamics of the project, but which also cannot be modified.

Regulations and Standards Compliance

In this section, which can be divided into two or more separate chapters, we describe all the implications arising from compliance with regulations and local / industry standards relating to the solutions proposed for reaching the project objectives and meeting its requirements.
However, this is not the place for a review of articles, subsections, circulars, references or laws, but rather for carefully considered analysis intended to illustrate how the project solutions – including the analysis and executive phases – comply with the dictates of applicable laws and de-facto, industry and legal standards.

This part of the project documentation must not be treated as a repetition of the definition of requirements, but contains explicit references to the proposed solutions and highlights how they comply with the relevant regulations.

If in doubt, it may help to consider requirements such as: "Fire Prevention Regulations" – the list of requirements would be uselessly long and misleading as compliance can be achieved through any number of methods and some will depend on project configurations. It is, however, extremely important to prepare a checklist to assist the Project Manager in supporting qualitative and quantitative verification of compliance with respect to such regulations.

Recently, the increasing number of authorities and certifying and regulatory bodies, mostly regarding the dynamics of the free market, has made it necessary to confirm the legitimacy of the actual Objectives in a project. Many businesses, usually the larger ones, have learned to use formulae (often tricky to evaluate) regarding the potential for "abuse of market dominance".

Clearly, given that even the outline analysis and design phases have costs that are often relevant, one should not arrive at this point due to the conclusions of the outline design, but rather one should evaluate the congruity of a proposal – project – with regulatory requirements to determine if any of the project objectives is unreachable due to incompatibility with laws.

It is advisable, therefore, in such rare cases, to follow the Objective definitions phase with a preliminary legal inspection phase regarding their legality.

It is crucial to perform a timely analysis of the regulatory context regarding projects that will be taking place in other countries, or on an international scale and thus subject to international laws and treaties that may be obscure, or very difficult to follow.

Some major enterprises have set up *supply chain* solutions while ignoring the key implications relating to applicable regulations regarding worker safety, resulting in huge efforts to analyse and complete a design that subsequently proved impossible to implement due to conflicts with certain health and safety requirements.

Furthermore, the more influential and pervasive regional regulations in federal states suggest dedicating a specific portion of this section of the project documentation to showing how the project complies with local regulations.

This can be of particular importance during any negotiation phases with local public bodies for obtaining authorisations and for announcements.

It is not unheard-of for even major construction projects to go through laborious and expensive modifications in order to comply with regional regulations.

Criticalities and Attention Points

This section is dedicated to those individual elements, mostly endogenous, that are capable of identifying certain difficulties with the correct implementation of the project.

For example, a project where the outcome is linked to a single supplier, the reliability of which has not been tested over time and for which the backup production capacity is also unknown, this section would be the correct place to highlight such issues.

In general, this section is where you would raise issues regarding potential dangers, or weaknesses in the general planning.

Returning to our earlier example, it would be strongly advisable to explain the necessity to perform an immediate market analysis for the purpose of identifying alternative suppliers. In other words, it is better to pre-emptively solve potential problems if they will be difficult, or even impossible, to resolve later in a timely manner.

Risk Management

There are many type of risks that may affect the project. Classic examples of risks a Project may be exposed to are:

- Natural disasters.
- The loss of key skills.
- Price volatility of key resources.
- Exchange rate fluctuation.
- Political instability and subsequent instability of regulatory frameworks.
- Suppliers or clients reliability.
- Change of market or other key environmental conditions.

The overall project risk is also a function of how innovative or unique the project is as well as of the magnitude of risks effects.

It is no surprise that risk identification, evaluation, and management are particularly complex for those organizations, such as the NASA, that are commonly involved in unique and extremely expensive Projects.
NASA's eight-step Risk Management framework incorporates the US Air Force Risk Matrix that is a remarkably clear starting point to understand how risks are evaluated and classified. It implies risks classification based on:

- Severity, that represents the magnitude of risk occurrence in terms of its effects according to a scale ranging from Catastrophic to Negligible, passing through Critical and Moderate.

- Probability, to which may be assigned the value Frequent, Likely, Occasional, Seldom, or Unlikely.

Following such classification, for each severity-probability combination, each risk can be classified from "Very High", if its Probability is Frequent and its Severity is Catastrophic, to Low, Probability=Unlikely and Severity=Negligible.

The US Air Force as well treats its missions like projects evaluating alternatives according to the result of the application of its risk management framework thus evaluating the overall risk of mission as the sum of each individual risk.

Typically, the "*Risk Assessments*" or "*Risk Identifications*" is the initial stage of the "*Risk Management Plan*". An enumeration of the dangers is performed with the goal of calculating the potential repercussions and, above all, to prepare in advance the formal countermeasures in what is usually known as the "*Risk Response Plan*".

According to Haimes (Haimes, 2009), risk management is based on the correspondence summarized in the following table.

Risk Assessment	Risk Management
"What can go wrong?"	"What can be done?"
"What is the likelihood that something will go wrong?"	"What are the available options and their associated tradeoffs?"
"What are the associated consequences?"	"What are the impacts of current decisions to future options?"

From the above, the section dedicated to *risk management* should be split into two sub-sections. One section should be dedicated to *Risk Identification* and the other should explain the planned countermeasures for which the most accurate term seems to that given by the PMBOK as "*Risk Response Plan*". Additionally, some cases may require their own section dedicated to "*Risk Cost Management*", presenting the procedures and related costs for activating the associated mitigation measures, or recovery procedures.

The writing of the *Risk Management Plan*, particularly where it describes the various incidences on costs and potential success of the project, should be done as a team. The Project Manager will access every competency available within the working group, within the wider group of stakeholders and, if necessary, with input from outside experts, with the goal of guaranteeing the reliability and completeness of the plan.

This is, however, why the Sponsor will take advantage of a Project Manager competent skilled in project planning in that he must, in any case, provide difficult assessments in order to provide reliable numbers for potential additional project costs, and also on the related probabilities.

For obvious reasons, the principal audience for the *Risk Management Plan* is the Sponsor.

It is worth underlining that Risk Management may greatly influence project. In recent times, after risk assessment and evaluation, a growing number of Project Plans have been dramatically modified in order to mitigate their overall exposure to risks. For example, following an analysis of a statistically relevant streak of disasters that ultimately led to financial disasters, in a growing number of projects implying complex, multi-tier supply chains involving interactions among and with suppliers spread all around the globe, the traditional cost-cutting oriented approach, that characterized the last thirty year at the turn of the century, left the way to a more careful sophisticated approach. According to this increasing sensitivity toward the potentially disruptive impact of risks, procurement and financial departments are more and more involved in risk evaluation than in the past.

Example: In 2001, I was a member of the team charged with distributing the new currency, the Euro, throughout Italy, which took place thanks to a dedicated supply chain and using a widespread distribution process that saw the execution, over four months, of over 120.000 deliveries of heavy, bulky handling units of considerable value, to around 42.000 delivery points spread across the country, as well as the mobilisation of a huge number of people and resources.

At one point during the distribution process, one of the ships transporting the metal for minting the coins was running very late and also, due to problems with satellite communications, it was impossible to obtain updates of its location. As you can imagine, this caused much alarm. Fortunately, it was not the only ship we had available for such transport duties and it incurred a delay that, while still critical, could be absorbed by boosting the downstream processes.
What would have happened if it had been decided to provide only a single ship, and said ship had failed to reach its destination?
It is worth pointing out that going with a single ship, where possible, was the better option from a cost perspective, but also the most risky in terms of project timing.
This is just one example of risk analysis that, while potentially fatal to the success of the project, points to a revision of the production process, despite the increase in total costs.

Risk Identification

As discussed previously, the identification of risks, is not carried out by the Project Manager herself. Instead, her role is to assign the task of identifying risks, calculating their probabilities of occurrence, and evaluating their repercussions on the project to industry experts. Obviously, a PM with a specific expertise in the field of the project may better provoke experts and challenge their assumptions scanning across stakeholders for further opinions or screening previous experiences for more insights.

It is crucial to explain immediately the value of an iterative approach to risk analysis.
This, in fact, should not be the last act of project planning, as it potentially informs the structure of project's activities.

The identification of a risk based on the reading of the project plan can lead to a revision of the latter to mitigate said risk. For this reason, the "*Risk Response Plan*" will be subjected to revision cycles particularly when the program, the context, or sequence of events is modified.

The classification of risks can be subjected to an initial division very similar to that found in software engineering, differentiating exceptions from errors. That is, an initial, very important, separation of two types of risks: those that, upon further investigation prove to have relatively easy solutions, from those that are impossible to mitigate against in advance with any guarantee of success.
For this reason, major projects require considerable investments and operate in contexts with identifiable unstable elements, require this section to be divided into at least two subsections:

- Primary Risks

Such risks have no valid mitigation, besides that of saving that which is salvageable. For example, there might be high risks of imminent armed conflicts in the area where the project is to take place, or natural disasters, etc.

- Secondary Risks
  These are manageable risks that require planning for said management in order to develop mitigation/recovery measures.

An example of a secondary risk is the possibility that one of the Team Leaders – one with very rare skills, perhaps – decides to leave his job for some reason, resulting in an undefined period of time during which the Team Leader's position is unfilled, resulting in the potential for disrupting the project's success.

The skill of the Project Manager is in knowing how to identify fully the most important risks for a project.
The following summary can act as a rule of thumb for most projects as it covers the most common risks:

- Loss of key competencies that are difficult to find.
  The success of many projects relies on human resources that provide particular skills, such as designers, but also consultants and negotiators, any of whom might abandon the work for various reasons. A project that relies heavily on the use of a large number of "unique" skills is very risky as the chances of one of these skills may be lost is inherently high.

- Missing key skills in the work groups.
  It is often the case that some design elements, initially considered marginal, take on greater importance, or become recognised for their difficulty only in a later phase of the project. This means the

work group may require skilled personnel not originally thought necessary.

- Missing, or extreme delay, in supply of required goods or services.
  This possibility must, in the first instance, influencing the processes relating to procurement, informing the supply contracts of goods and services, and possible recovery actions if a supplier proves unable to meet their obligations. Remember that risks to which a supplier is exposed are project risks.

- Incorrect estimate of duration or difficulty of some tasks – perhaps because the task is innovative or has been insufficiently analysed.

- Advent of disruptive innovations affecting Project's goals or requirements.

Qualitative and Quantitative Risk Analysis

Nevertheless, one of the most interesting aspects of risk analysis lies in the potential to obtain a numerical evaluation of the overall project risk that can be considered, in some form, an identification of the project overall probability of success and support the forecast of a likely cost variance.
The following table suggests a possible form for a Risk Register.

Risk ID	Description	Mitigation Measures	Impact				Probability	Severity
			OBJ	Req	Task	Funct		
			Impacted Objective(s)	Impacted Requirement(s)	Impacted Task(s)	Impacted Functionalities	1-5 [6] Frequent Probable Occasional Remote Improbable [Eliminated]	1-4 Catastrofic Critical Marginal Negligible

Such a structure enables a numeric evaluation of the overall risk rating for project alternatives as a sum of individual probability and severity assigned to all risks.
Moreover, if the impact of every occurrence is carefully evaluated in terms of its potential effect on the achievement of Objectives, Requirements, Tasks, and Functionalities or Features, a more detailed analysis concerning the achievability of or attainability to such elements may be performed as a sum of i.e.:

(Importance of Requirement) X (Risk Probability) X (Risk Severity)

For all the risks impacting a specific requirement.

Previous experiences and extensive research play a fundamental role in gauging the probability of occurrence of a specific risk.

Another useful source of information could be recording the functional area from which the risk is originated (E.g. Human Resources, Operations, or Supplier x). This will enable or at least add new perspectives to the identification and weighting of organizational weaknesses thus stimulating further considerations concerning the Firm's or Institution's global fitness for the purpose.

Risk Response Plan

This is the most important, and most reassuring, part of the *Risk Management* section.
It consists of planning, and estimating cost, of measures and procedures that will mitigate the effects of risks occurrence.
It is effective – and highly recommended – to present the action plans in a graphical/tabular form too.

Technical Description of the Solutions

At this point, having produced a sufficiently clear vision of the solution from a feature perspective, it is sufficient to illustrate the specific approaches and techniques to be applied, always with the assistance of schematics and diagrams, in language that is as jargon-free as possible.

This section should include the breakdown of the solution, along with the technical description explaining why specific choices were made at the design stage of each part, with links – ideally hyperlinks – to the detailed technical documents.

Execution Phase

Project Events

Every Project will (or should) go through the events depicted in the following image, which also exemplifies the succession and a frequency of such events.

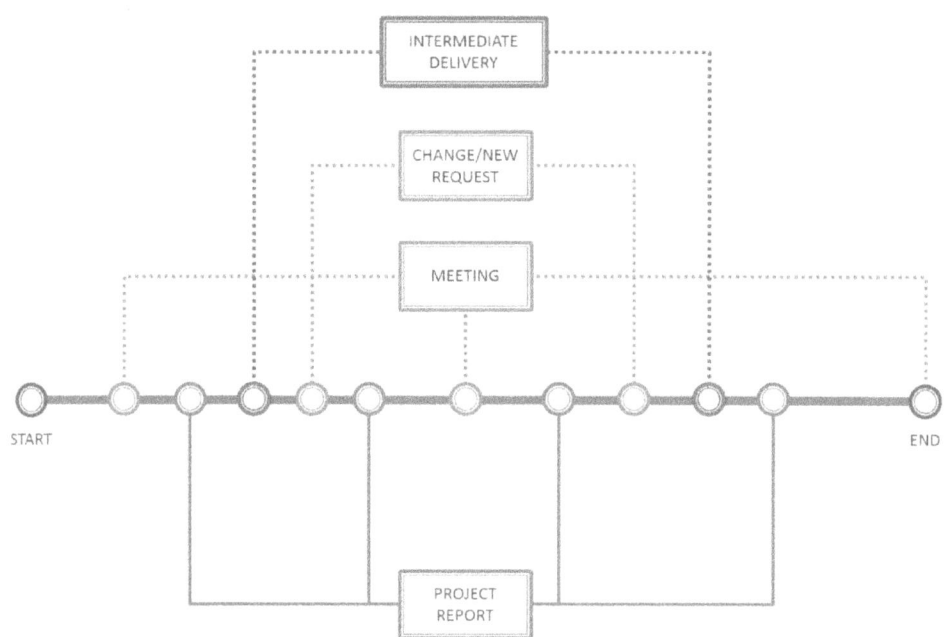

Picture 6

Meetings

A Project should start with an initial meeting presided by the Sponsor during which every Stakeholder should be represented.
The Sponsor should start underlining Project's Objectives, introducing the Project Manager and provide clear directives concerning his or her prerogatives within the Project.
During the initial meeting, the Sponsor and/or the PM should provide a thorough representation of the Project communication plan they had agreed upon.

Moreover, in order to minimize time waste and maximize project meetings effectiveness, not every Stakeholder should attend all of them, as only directly interested people should be invited; therefore, the Sponsor and the PM should also clarify about meeting attendance criteria.

Except for the first and the last Project meeting, the PM is usually responsible for conducting the meeting. It will have a precise scope defined through a list of topics, a list of participants and an expected duration.

As said, during the Project development, the Project Manager will convene targeted meetings, oriented to the discussion of very specific topics and therefore only directly interested Stakeholders will be called to attend. The circumstance will ensure meeting effectiveness due the limited number of participants and their specific knowledge on covered topics.

Because a clear definition of Meeting agenda is a key prerequisite of an effective meeting, in order to ensure that all participants will be aware of the subjects of the meeting and be prepared for the discussion, PM will better share with them a fairly detailed agenda in advance.

However, the most important prerequisite for a meeting is that it has to be necessary. To demonstrate that a PM works and has control over the project is not useful for the Project. Therefore, to respect for others' time, if there is no real need for it the PM would better do not call the meeting. Information about Project progress will be collected as further described talking about Project Tracking and will be delivered as described below concerning the Project Report.

Conducting a meeting is not an easy task! It requires experience and specific communication skills and qualities somehow related to negotiation skills in order to command people's attention and keep the discussion on track or even to deal with difficult-to-manage behaviors.

Conducting meetings is undoubtedly the far most challenging task for a rookie Project Management. Therefore, in order to minimize the risk of conflicts and unexpected reactions a prior confrontation with the involved parts is highly. Such a survey will increase PM's ability to anticipate conflicts and provide her/him with relevant information concerning opinions, tensions or ideas thus making her/him more prepared for the discussion.

Here are some suggested guidelines to be followed during a meeting:

Start underlining the scope.
Involve everyone in the discussion. That means do not let anyone leave the mining without having expressed her/his opinion.
Up to a point, give everyone the opportunity to express himself or herself. This, as we will discuss in the appendix about psychology, not only means expressing ideas and concepts that are directly related to meeting subjects. The success of a meeting is highly related to PM's ability to make everyone feel at ease.
Close with an action plan specifying purposes, assignments and deadlines or expected dates.

Relevant information that emerged from the discussion will be summarized in a Meeting Report to be distributed according to the Communication Plan.
The essential elements of a Project Report are suggested as follows:

Thanks – Start the document thanking meeting participants for their contribution to the discussion.

Summarize meeting outcomes and findings.

Summarize the tasks (persons in charge) and the related deadlines or expected due dates.

For each Task underline its relation with Work-packages completion or Project success.

Close positively with motivational phrases. Motivation and positivity are essential for Project Success, especially in tough situations. Use sentences like: "the effort of Team A in order to find a compelling solution for this issue, as it happened in the case of …., will make Team B able to …., Team C offered its availability for phase 2 Tests".

As for any other Project related document, especially if they are targeted to top management, the ability to be succinct by synthesizing concepts will be greatly appreciated.

If the Project has been a success, celebrate it with a final meeting during which the PM and the Sponsor might recall Project challenges and tough times, thank Team members for their ability to overcome them and then cede the stage to them for their own moments of glory. During such event the Project Manager better limit herself or himself to coordinate speeches.

If the Project was a failure, or it was stopped at an early stage of development, a final meeting would be useful to clarify the reasons why the initiative failed and could turn into an important time for professional and human growth, even strengthening the link between the people and the organization.

Remember that stakeholders' opinion about Project Manager will be largely based on her/his ability to conduct meetings.

Project Report

The Project Report is a document issued by the PM on a regular basis, providing information about the Project progress.
The nature and extent of information contained in the Project Report may vary depending on the type of recipients according to Sponsor's preferences. Thus, the PM may release distinct Project Reports containing diverse combinations of relevant Project data. Most of the times, for instance, Project's financial data are made available to a very small audience. However, generally, the main recipient of the Project Report is the Sponsor and therefore, it is highly recommended to write it as short and as clear as possible; two pages length would be ideal. Having all Project Reports available in the same form is essential in order to make them comparable as well as to have the recipients familiar with the same information structure release after release. The purpose of the Project Report is to provide a snapshot of the progress of the initiative and therefore its content is supposed to be essential. The following structure is generally suitable.

- General progress against cost and time Baselines.
- Critical Issues (if any) – that is criticalities that must be addressed.
- Resolved Issues – that is issues that had been solved from the last release of the report.
- Overdue Work-packages – that is work-packages or critical Tasks that are behind schedule by the report release date, including possible recovery actions.
- Critical Changes from the start and/or from the last Report, including data about their possible impact on time, budget, resources and know-how.
- Relevant considerations or comments about the Project state.
- Eventual good notes, like remarkable Team performance or particularly brilliant contributions to the project progress.

Change Request e New Request

As said before, along its development the Project will likely change, hence change management has to be considered a normal activity for PMs. Projects normally pass through a series of unexpected change requests that may affect Project's Objectives, Requisites or Functionalities due to a variety of reasons.

The Project Manager is responsible for communicating and to a variable extent for managing the impacts of changes on the Project course. Such impacts may be scaring if changes will be related to Project's Objective, much less worrying if they would affect Requirements or possibly irrelevant in case they relate to Functionalities.

However, the correct, shared and well-documented management of changes is vital for the success of the initiative and therefore PM is responsible for:

1. Verifying the compatibility between changes and Project's Objectives. In particular if changes relate to Objectives, PM should perform an accurate revision of Project Plan in order to ensure such compliance.

2. Overseeing changes approval, sharing and documentation.

Thus, it is mandatory that Changes will be evaluated in a collegial manner and following a compelling, predefined flow.

Moreover, it is essential that Changes will be approved following an equally formalized and agreed workflow and that their approval result in adequate changes in the Project documentation.

Also in this case the keywords are sharing and documenting.

Tracking

By tracking a project, we refer to the tracing of the progress of activities compared to the most recent approved baseline.
We briefly discussed about the two essential interdependent time and cost baselines.
There are two ways of Tracking a Project: Centralized and Delegated.
Centralized Tracking is performed by the PM, normally using Project Management Tools or Systems (PMT or PMS), by registering the progress of single Tasks or entire work-packages indicating their percentage of completion. Through such input, because each Task is characterized by a specific pool of resources whose unit cost is also specified, Project Management Tools may provide any kind or analysis and chart related time and cost trends.
However, we should ask ourselves how the PM could possibly be aware of the real progress of Teams' and individuals' activity.
I have direct experience of Projects during which PMs overwhelmed Teams and individuals with continuous, stressful request for detailed information concerning their activities in order to gain indicators about their real progress, thus transforming the role of PM to that of an unbearable accountant auditor. Such an activity is not only pointless; it is rather a form of sabotage.
The satisfaction of PM's needs in terms of information about Project progress should not turn into a strenuous activity for team-members. They do not work for the Project Manager herself; they work for the Project success. The work of a PM does not consist in a day-by-day tracking of Project activities. Moreover, especially if no partial/measurable or tangible results are available, there is no guarantee about the accuracy and reliability of such however indirectly collected progress data.

There is a very effective set of development techniques that could be adopted in order to assess and track Project progresses minimizing risks, which are essentially derived from Lean Manufacturing principles, based on iterative validation cycles starting from the definition of a so-called "Minimum Viable Product". Concerning Project Tracking, an essential characteristic of the Lean Methodology stands in its appeal to strong prototyping and consistent incremental development cycles with a systematic recourse to measurable – even though partial - results as soon as possible. Such early measures may concern the adherence to Objectives or the customer satisfaction or acceptance of a product or service, and then become precious feedbacks serving as inputs for subsequent development phases hence minimizing the weight of wrong hypothesis and therefore significantly reducing risks.

Thus, the more the project is innovative and/or challenging and expensive the ability of a PM to master lean techniques and therefore to design Strategic Project Plans will constitute a great competitive advantage for her or him as well as for the served organization.

Delegate Tracking, is a form of high involvement management, as it consists in delegating Project Tracking to the people in charge for project activities.

If on the one hand, this approach is proven to empower associates making them more aware of their role as part of a whole and accountable for their results; on the other hand, it requires greater professionalism and exposes the organization to late surprises in case of individual or Team wrong indications of their real progress.

Therefore, although Delegated Tracking is generally proven more effective than Centralized Tracking, its application should be better coupled with lean techniques in case of highly innovative initiatives or when the project requires a large recourse to external resources whose affordability have never been tested before.

In general terms, the application of Delegated Tracking avoids the perception of the PM as an accountant auditor, promotes Team and individuals engagement and accountability, discouraging mendacious reporting of activities progress but, more importantly.

Information on Project progress is the essential component of a Project Report; therefore, especially in the case of Delegated Tracking it should be constantly available on a GANTT on a Project website. Such measure will increase associates' awareness of being part of a bigger picture and of what their role is within such picture.

Given a Project Plan, with Tasks' individual resources and estimated duration, to a given delay will generally correspond a higher cost, while in case Tasks are globally ahead of schedule it will result in lower a cost. The sum of individual costs of each Task is usually referred to with the term Earned Value, and it will be positive in case of savings, or negative when the overall Project cost exceeds the budgeted or baseline cost.

As mentioned, once specified the cost and the nature – essentially variable of fixed - of each resource as well as their usage for each Task, given Tracking data, Project Management Tools may provide a variety of automated trend analysis and statistics that would support decisions concerning the impact of delays and possible recovery actions.

Closing a Project

It is hoped that the conclusion of a project involves acknowledgements and satisfaction.
The Project Manager should openly thank the Teams, the Sponsors, and anyone else who has contributed to the success of the initiative.
If this is not the case – e.g. if the project has been interrupted – this should still become part of the internalised knowledge base of the organisation.
For this purpose, the latter should guarantee the availability of the project documentation, while the PM should write up a report explaining the reasons for the failure of the project.

Appendix A: Psychology

It is clear that, besides those rare cases deserving of clinical analysis, none of us should ignore our loves, families, or ourselves.
It is now well known that good managers, who know how to network, know how to negotiate successfully and know how motivate their teams to obtain the best results, must have mature skills similar to those of a psychologist.
In fact, such managers are likely to face obstacles and difficulties that have nothing to do with the nature of the project itself, such as difficult workers, stakeholder conflicts, etc.

I make no pretence of seeing this argument as a scientific paper, nor is it particularly analytical; there are plenty of excellent texts on the subject, some of which we have remembered to include in the bibliography. But it is necessary to remind readers that, in the absence of an adequate psychological grounding or rather, due to the psychological implications of working in groups, the exercise of leadership and negotiation both, Project Managers and team leaders alike, are very likely to fail, either totally or partially, even if they are otherwise very highly qualified at a technical level.

The knowledge collected on the subject, and good books, have allowed us to summarise the few elementary principles the observance of which can greatly assist in the work of the Project Manager, as follows:

Appendix B: Managing Teams and the Need to express one's personality

With this last definition, I intend to clarify the most common cause of apparently incomprehensible reactions and behaviours. These are usually undesirable, certainly useless and in any case not helping the smooth, correct running of the activities. Such behaviours sometimes trigger conflicts or strong antipathies, capable of prejudicing the achievement of the project objectives.

What it is: briefly, it's a form of insecurity, or – if you prefer – a sense of inadequacy, which leads to a need to express oneself, to impose one's personality, or for one's role in the team to be recognised, legitimised, duly considered, or reappraised.

This need, originating from a point of weakness, originates from insecurities and / or frustration, from the fear created by a sense of inadequacy for one's position. Conversely, this can occasionally stem from narcissism, or a superiority complex.

Each of you, when working in a team, has either already confronted – or will confront – behaviour stemming from the needs described above and ascribable to (I am definitely simplifying here) a need to express or impose one's personality.

Meetings are all too often subjected to such ranting, of dubious relevance to the topics under discussion. It is generally a defensive, often predictable, form of behaviour. A common form is: "Oh, aren't you all so very clever! Allow me to demonstrate who I am, before you get any ideas about my value [to this project / team]"

An older member of a team, having to confront the presence of younger, highly qualified and certified, members, and perhaps also the obsolescence of his own abilities, attempts to show how valuable he is by pointing at his "irreplaceable" wisdom. He tends to recount his countless experiences on older projects, often of minimal interest in the context of the topics being discussed and perhaps even artfully distorted or inflated, with the aim of underlining his value, or to avoid having some of his duties taken away from him.

Some female managers, who already find themselves discriminated against when applying for such roles, tend to become arrogant, even openly and aggressive in appearing resolute and disproportionally decisive, leading to brusque behaviour bordering on rudeness and often making decisions too hastily, requiring review. This seems particularly common in Latin countries. A typical outburst might be: "*I'll show you what a great leader I am! I could command a platoon of marines!*"

Occasionally, some managers, often indecisive, or those lacking specific or adequate skills, cultivate an abstract or archaic notion of wanting to "be valued". These tend to express a particular aggression, raising their voice and using a confrontation tone, often well before an argument should happen, in an attempt to affirm their leadership in a crude, almost physical, manner.

Or take the younger manager, technically very prepared, but with a tendency to retort in a mocking, sarcastic tone to observations about their work or decisions. This is, however, a primarily diplomatic concern, and the Project Manager must become standard bearer and inspiration for the group, in addition to exercising diplomacy directly, something that will be touched upon briefly below.

Similar behaviours can certainly cause loss of time and may trigger personal conflicts fed by contrasting weaknesses.
Still, we should consider that some release, within acceptable limits, of such behaviours not only brings a little humanity into the project, but also is also inevitable. Furthermore, it need not be a negative process, but can even help people understand each other better and enter

into confidences. It is rewarding for the bearer; it calms them down.

It is only necessary to know that some behaviours are not permitted by the Project Manager and that, in general, an expert professional, balanced, secure in himself, will not apply them. He has no need, and can label them as originating from his weaknesses.

Generally, being able to withstand an aggressive rant by remaining impassive, but not contemptuous, and then being firm, calm and, where possible, conciliatory, is a very good starting point.

A rule? Let those who have the need to vent do so, and try to alleviate his problems, even if, most times, this last has nothing to do with the project itself. Never try to act openly like a psychologist; don't give life lessons; know how to listen – better if in another location.

There is also a set of behaviours similar to those listed that more experienced managers use to measure reactions, but that's another story!

For more in-depth information about the themes discussed here, we recommend reading books on the subject of negotiation.
For brevity and effectiveness, we suggest reading "Winning Negotiations" (Harvard Business Press) and, from the same series, "Managing Difficult Interactions".

A rule? When faced with inappropriate, or improper, behaviour, try to avoid applying your authority and, instead, take a calm and conciliatory approach. If possible, show that you understand the reasons for the behaviour and give them a second chance, provided that they respond positively and show interest in resolving the problem.

Appendix C – Summary of Project Documentation Contents

		LOGICAL LAYER	CONTENT	DOCUMENT TYPE		
PROJECT	ANALYSIS	DEFINITION	BACKGROUND AND DESCRIPTION OF THE CONTEXT	BACKGROUND	ASSESSMENT	CONCEPT - VISION
				PROJECT SCOPE		
				ASSESSMENT		
			DESCRIPTION OF THE PROBLEM	OBJECTIVES / BENEFITS	BUSINESS CASE	
				REQUIREMENTS		
				CONSTRAINTS		
		SOLUTION OUTLINE	FUNCTIONAL DESCRIPTION OF PROPOSAL	GENERAL DESCRIPTION OF PROPOSAL	PROJECT PLAN	MASTER PLAN
				USE CASES / PROCESS MAPS		
				DESCRIPTION OF FUNCTIONALITIES/FEATURES		
			PLANNING AND ORGANIZATION	GENERAL DESCRIPTION OF THE SOLUTION		
				ACTIVITIES AND PHASES		
				TEAMS / EQUIPMENT / INFRASTRUCTURES		
				FINANCIAL ANALYSIS - BUDGETING		
				EXTERNAL CONSTRAINTS AND ASSUMPTIONS		
			RISKS AND CRITICAL TO SUCCESS ELEMENTS AND FACTORS	STANDARDS AND REGULATIONS		
				ATTENTION POINTS		
				RISK MANAGEMENT		
	TECHNICAL DESIGN		TECHNICAL DESCRIPTION OF PROPOSAL	PROTOTYPING	TECHNICAL DESIGN	
				DETAILED DESIGN		
				QUALITY PLAN		
				TEST PLAN		

Appendix D – Connections between basic entities and Project

Process for identifying and linking, intended for inspections, summarised representations, and monitoring. The consistent link between entities is essential to provide a compelling picture of the Project as a whole. As said Function may be read feature or functionality.

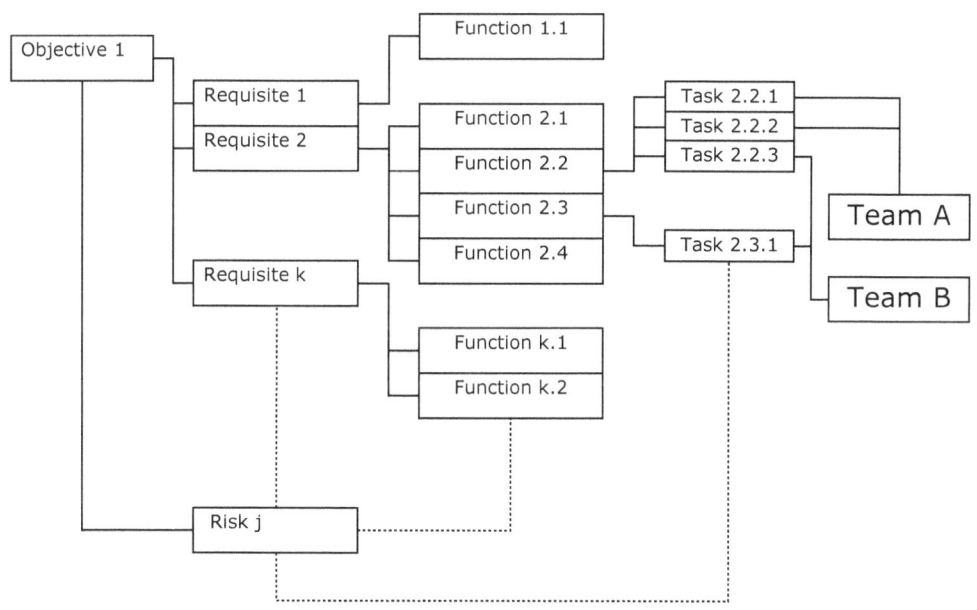

Bibliography

Haimes, Y. Y. (2009). *Risk Modeling, Assessment, and Management.* Hoboken, NJ (USA): Wiley.

Harvard Business School Press. (2003). *Managing Projects Large and Small: The Fundamental Skills to Deliver on budget and on Time.* Cambridge, Massachussetts, USA: Harvard Business School Press.

Harvard Business School Press. (2008). *Managing Difficult Interactions.* Cambridge, Massachussetts, USA: Harvard Business School Press.

Hitt, M. A., Miller, C. C., & Colella, A. -T. (2010). *OB - Organizational Behavior.* Hoboken, New Jersey, USA: John Wiley & Sons Inc.

Office of Government Commerce. (2009). *Managing Successful Projects with PRINCE2.* Norwich, England, UK: The Stationery Office on behalf of Office of Government Commerce.

Project Management Institute. (2013). *A Guide to the Project Management Body of Knowledge.* Newtown Square, Pennsilvanya, USA: Project Management Institute, Inc.

About the Author

Raffaello Leti Messina was born in Rome in 1969. He obtained a master degree of Urban & Land Planning, specialising in eco-energetic land planning and then he has been awarded a Strategic Management Certificate from Harvard University.

In 1996, he began his professional career as freelance consultant for major corporations and international institutions in the field of land analysis, distributed process design and optimization, GIS and eco-energetic land planning.

In 2001, he was appointed by the Italian Postal Service responsible for planning and monitoring applications enabling operations related to the distribution of the newly adopted Euro currency to approximately 28.000 bank agencies and 14.400 post offices, as well as for data reporting to the Central Bank and the Ministry of Treasuries.

He has an extensive experience in managing complex projects, analysing modelling and optimising distributed processes.

Starting from 2003 he has been appointed as CEO of several consulting firms.

He is co-founder and currently CEO of Consulenze Progetti Sviluppo S.r.l.

Raffaello is also MBA Professor of Project Management and MBA Professor of Production Processes and Logistics at Link University Campus.

www.ingramcontent.com/pod-product-compliance
Lightning Source LLC
Chambersburg PA
CBHW071800170526
45167CB00003B/1103